Bottled Ganges
Replacing the handmade version

Yogesh Patel

Skylark Publications UK
10 Hillcross Avenue, Morden, Surrey SM4 4EA
www.skylarkpublications.co.uk

First Edition: Bottled Ganges

First published in Great Britain in 2008 by:
Skylark Publications UK
10 Hillcross Avenue
Morden, Surrey SM4 4EA
www.skylarkpublications.co.uk

ISBN 978-0-9560840-0-2

Designed and typeset by Skylark Publications UK. Printed and bound in Great Britain and through various channels internationally to be printed locally and distributed

By the same author:
BOOKS:
The Manikin In Exile, a collection of poems in English
Magic Glasses, A children's picture book in English
Rough Guide Phrasebook, Hindi, for the famous PENGUIN series
Ahin, a collection of poems in Gujarati
Pagalani Lipi, a collection of short stories in Gujarati

RECORDS:
Teri Yaad Aayee, Hindi
Geet and Gazals, Hindi
Tahukar, Gujarati
Door-kinara, Gujarati

FILMS/RADIO PLAYS:
The Last Days Of Gandhi, in English, Kumbho Films
Companions Forever, BBC Radio 4

As a co-editor of Skylark, **Yogesh Patel** has published international contemporary poetry since the seventies. Currently, he runs Skylark Publications UK and a non-profit **Word Masala** project to promote writers and poets of the South Asian diaspora. Recently he launched a South-Asian 'Poet of the month' e-zine series. Yogesh is also a founder of the *literary charity*, Gujarati Literary Academy, and has served as its president. He was a Fellow of the International Poetry Society and a Fellow of the Royal Society of Arts. He was awarded *the Freedom of the City of London* and has four LP records, two films, radio programmes, children's books, fiction and non-fiction books, including poetry collections to his credit.

Apart from being a recipient of the IWWP award, the International Scottish Diploma for excellence in poetry, Vatayan International Award for the Excellence in Poetry in the House of Lords and a Hon. Diploma from the Italian University of Arts, he has received the Co-Op Award for the poetry on the environment.

By profession, Yogesh is a qualified optometrist and an accountant.

A short list of his work and achievements are listed at
www.patelyogesh.co.uk

(His collection of poems, *Swimming with Whales,* was published in 2017. He has been published in PN Review, The London Magazine, Shearsman, Under the Radar, IOTA, Envoi, Fire, Orbis, IPSE, BBC, Asian Literary Review, Muse India, Confluence, Asian Voice, Skylark, and others. He is also anthologised in MacMillan, Redbeck and other anthologies. He has read at many prestigious venues, including the House of Lords and the National Poetry Library, Southbank.)

Dedicated to

Skylark Magazine
*for serving poetry with 100 issues
at journey's end*

*

Asian Voice
&
Gujarat Samachar (London)
for an uncompromising bold journalism

Bottled Ganges

A revised version

The original publication was a handmade computer book: an experiment.
This version replaces it and corrects typos. We will replace your original copy free

Skylark Publications UK

Thank you for your sponsorship

Index

Bottled Ganges

I bottled the Ganges
and set the sails
in the quest of Ré
on the banks of the Nile
With Mokele of Lake Tumba
and Nkombe, the Mongo warrior
I shared the hookah
While for the bottled Ganges
I elevated a temple
Mokele stole the sun
Nkombe opened God's gift on the horizon
They danced as the first light came
"The sun's found, the sun's found!"
But then they came in their army uniforms
Alas, kicked out were we
the bottled Ganges and I

On the banks where Canute sat once
I tried to wash off my sin
my greatest crime: my skin

I wash not with Canute's river
I wash not with bottled Ganges
but in the devil's dream
I'm doomed to do with the rivers of blood

I refuse to be consumed
A skinhead throws a stone at me
to smash the bottled Ganges

I run, run, and run
like a rat in the subterranean castle
I still carry the burden of this bottle

I dilute it with tap water
And lo! I drink it
In the communion, dilute it I more
and share, and share...
The Ganges unleashed as a genius
swells and swells; knows no bounds

Such arrogance! It mocks its own mother

Engulfed I look for my name
at Thoth's Heliopolis, the mound at Khemenu
in Ayodhya, Kurukshetra and Ashoka's Kaling
in the streets of Brixton and Tottenham

Alas, I'm nothing but the bloody skin

The skin is a passport
The skin is a number
The passport's tattooed with a number
The number, the essence, has no flesh, no bones

With such a legacy, I tell my son, "I'm waiting
I'm waiting for Prajapati to utter

'BHUR', so I can find earth
'BHUVAH', so I can find the air
and 'SVAH', so I can have the sky
Then I can begin
I can give thee the hope
The plain for the sun to rise on
and the Ganges to come down to

Until then, this is it
hang it around your neck

Baboon's Bacon

Lo! Baboon found a pen
He wants to write
He wants to be famous
He wants to laugh at others
He wants to show he is not a monkey

He wants you to know he is an owl
Most wise, the only intellectual, well poised
Not Ted Hughes's Crow
The (only) voice of God

Enter another enterprising baboon
And lo! He lands his two rear bacon
What a racket
Now they have a newspaper

Baboon monkeys around words happily ever after
Next comes banana
To wipe words on the shiny bacon
Written, rewritten, rubbed, and written again
A child's writing tablet
Oh! What a racket!
Words win; no *chuddies*

Next time you are in a jungle
Don't trust a whisper in the air
Shush, shush, not a word from you, please

For baboons are also
The custodians of
Freedom of Speech

Morning Dew

1.

Eyes penetrate
heavily fogged words

Everything explained
while in Kumbhkarna's slumber
only to find
a war
between the sun and a newspaper

2.

I am born
from a tube station
every morning
for hope

I see the clouds of blank faces about
whispers, whispers
a market of words
stalls after stalls of the wordmongers,
words of Obamas and Osamas
coloured by the artists in Fleet Street

The light, all fake
not of the sun
A suicide bomber
pours his last Starbucks' coffee on my hope

The Bhagavad Gita
leafs through the city pages
to find today's price of hope

3.

न तत्र सूर्यॊ भाति
Until the sun is born
Until the sun is born
Until the sun is born

ॐ सूर्य देवाय नमः
Ohm Sury Devaay Namah
(I thee bow, oh Sun)

न तत्र सूर्यॊ भाति
Until the sun is born
Until the sun is born
Until the sun is born

!

The Pigeon Droppings

I have taken the poison
but I'm not Shiva
I have caught the Ganges in my hair
but I'm not Mahadeva

I haven't drunk up the sea

I have no claims over any heavens
or the real Truth

nor have I any godly acts to dance Tandava to

I am simply
a broken statue of Mahatma Gandhi
on a hunger strike
for decades

on which
rains
pigeon droppings
non-stop

Totally Damaged

I never told the sea to rise
gobble up the sun
or play with any moon
No, I never indulged

If you overindulge yourself like Ghalib
If you throw up
lose the sun
then live with it; not my problem

The sea should have known better
The sun is not a marble

My game is to be a stone
a stone god
If ever anyone tried to split
a coconut on my head
as the Hindu ritual goes
at least, I would have avoided the hurt

Until then I remain a poet
totally damaged

With the statistical skin and a given heart

Let words drag me to a trial
again and again

A Slipped Hand (1)

God had only extended His hand
to bless the man

But the man exploded
as a suicide bomber
Embracing him
God shouting to his deaf ears
'Holy Book is not greater than God'

Blast!
God's hand all burnt
shaky

His words are now
dragged lines of fire
on a crimson canvas
hanging over a city raped violently

A depot's statue crumbling to rubble
Still a smile on his face:
'One day I shall have my day
Fools are many
Religion is greater than God.'

A Slipped Hand (2)

The injured God is at a loss
When did He cut off his thumb
passed it on to a man
posing as Dhronacharya?

He knows now why there is no more
His thumbprint on the world

A man knows He can't hold a pen
Hence, the words
are nothing but
garbled drag marks
on a bloody sky...

A Slipped Hand (3)

Who is the culprit?
Who has dragged heavy lines of light
on a polished glass of sky
punctuated with aeroplanes
hovering vultures
in the sky
above a hapless
thunderously coughing
city?
Boom, boom.

Come, come
Watch the spectacles of words
hanging like a dark cloud of smoke
over the city gang-raped by the politics

The one who ignites the fire knows:
Man invented the words
God only spoke them as commanded!

God and the Translator

God is butted out of the holy book
'Get lost!'
A translator has run away with His words
God is ordered to prove Himself to man

Hiding His words in his turban
the latest Alibaba wanders the deserts
Now he is a conjurer of mesmerising words

Poor God!
He wouldn't say, He couldn't say
He has no words

The translator has pushed him back in the womb, hard
Crow is finally the winner
Crow pretends to be Krishna
The unborn God is Abhimanyu
Crow tells Him the lies
If He is born as a man
He can blow up Himself
And of course others
Before the seventh war-zone

God has no solution
He is not taught the trick to escape
Crow's game

God knows not
He is Abhimanyu
Therefore
He will never get out alive

The translator has trapped Him for good

Windermere in the Evening

The gulls drag the sky away, heavy
Air; foul with the smell of a dead lake
but better than the smell of gutters
locked in my drawer

No one helps the sinking sun
in a shop-window

The streets have the silence of anticipation
waiting for the curtain to lift

The drama:
The sun is a phantom on this stage
My face, a wooden mask
Who's dead?
Yes, yes, it's a street theatre
Antony's speech after Caesar's death
on deaf ears
The long silence has words
stretched like roads with road signs
that no one reads

I throw the hoop of M25 in the lake
No sound
The moon decides to float on it
Gulls take away the sky
No drama, no spotlights, no curtains
A resurrection
Come, come to Windermere
To watch the silly moon
The drowning sun

No questions asked...

A Dialogue

Million years across the table

Only one real red rose in the flower vase

We both have our hands stretched
full of thorns

The tablecloth is a monument

A mammoth bone on the table has
windy words trapped

Grey emptiness lying stark naked in its
ripe curves
on artist's blank canvas

I have no red rose and you don't want one

A stretched ice between us
on this table
with the sculptures of words

Trickery

A morning stunned by the snow
A feather woke up the sky
From the vacuity of the words
took off bosom's hollowness.
A brush of silence dabbed the rainbow
and sang a song in colours magical
But where is this smell from
of the flesh roasting?
A cannibal at work?

A lost snow-rabbit is madly
searching for leaves

I know our love is formal
of the feathers ruffled
of the dislodged
gliding
falling snow
or is it the snow riding the morning?

The darkness wants to escape
a silent emptiness of my bones
Jumping out it wants to play snowballs

I slightly pushed open the window
And lo! The skin flaked off

Just look at the trickery!
Rattling the keys
the sun appeared at the door
and you

God, what do we do now?
We are total strangers

Words

words are dead skylarks
words are the Sahara
words are burning firewood
words are a poet's leftover warbling
words are prostitutes
words are theirs, not mine
words are white tablecloths
words are flower vases
words are dogs of war
words are Socrates' poison
words are passports and virginity tests
words are the rivers of blood
words are Dali's melting clocks, fused, wired

words are also poetry
and poetry can defuse the bomb

but religion is a firewall

A Role Play

I have never
walked the walk with you
without the seas emptied in me
by you

Given a chance
I would have enjoyed
to share a depth inside me

I have never been able to walk
with the sun
without being totally blinded by it

Given a chance
I would have
been blessed with the brightness

Only if I had been
able to walk with me

and with you
and with a rose
I would have enjoyed words

The Table and Us

between our eyes
the expanse of the nothingness of our eyes

between our words
the amplitude of uncommunicative words

between us
etherised whiteness
the endless beach
the frozen sea
a blank A4
a dead cuckoo
a table

a polished void

this side, that side

centripetal eyes, words, voids, silence
centrifugal us

The Curse

there was a curse called the sky
the senseless bird didn't know
oh, the pride of the wings!
but for how long?

in the end, the bird died
no one noticed
no one knew
no one asked
oh, but the pride of the wings!
but what now?

the curse called sky is there
-still-
for you
for me

A Tale

an old man recounts:

we used to have roses
Himalayan honeysuckles
fiery butterflies
peacocks, blackbirds, cuckoos
the rain, the snow, and the wrath of the sun

the children
under the spell of a General
with guts open on the blasting mines
or labouring as slaves
reach out for Dali's melting clock
throw it at the old man's face
and holler:

a bloody liar!

Future

an old man said:

in the good old days
there were birds
beautiful
colourful
chanting sweet songs

the children
accustomed to warplanes
stared at him
with eyes wide, disbelieving
then exploded:

rogue! he is a liar!

The Metaphysical City

the cities are like Ariadne
Ahalya
the roads stretching out like the black tongues
eager to hoop round Joseph K's neck
people are invisible apparitions
no voice, face, eyes, or skin
pavement's expecting hand
stretched to the horizon
the silence trapped between light and shadow
the furniture has grown wings
hope is carried by the scrap collector
Orestes pursued by Furies is found safe in the temple
like the manikin bereft of love
a blind man who looked in Re's eyes is waiting to lead
crushed under the stacked up apartment
dreams on trial in the court of light
the mutation of a man
meanders to fit the mosaic of metaphysical relativity

only the container of the Big Mac
existentially
home!

Metaphysical Landscapes 1 and 2

A Journey through a Metaphysical Canvas

strained silhouettes
the wrinkles on a face
the lines mist
the bounds unshackle
the imprisonment
a trapped space oscillates
the colours turn to ashes
the fire pants
the residue
the asphalt's drab
breaks the shell

the words run to the church
ring the bells
time laughs

in the cloudy square
under the glass sky
the ghosts of children play
with the ball of cold sun

I'm a passer-by
a manikin on the metaphysical canvas
in search of boundaries to cross

A Strange City

Along the barren roads of reality
amidst the eyes like traffic lights
with a glow-worm in a heart
in the landscape of hostile dreams
I've fed my soul to a pale sun
Here has been my game
on a grey canvas
where manikins live in a dab of colour
where they quarrel with their incongruity
and monuments of lies

The space to breathe
is a paper tablecloth spread between us
Only the nylon flowers struggle to put a meaning
in this timeless void stretching endlessly
primaeval gunge of nothingness
Even a fresh rose has no voice here
Yet, it's an interior decorator's perfection
A perfect designer silence
A sculpted purpose fulfilled. Moksha

The manikin civilisation
The manikin's glasshouse
No entry. No exit

A poet tosses the stones
gods, words and love
Yes, I was tossed in Africa
had my genes toasted in India
and I'm rubber-stamped with Britannia

They see me of terracotta
a heap of Gorgon's slight
They came to colour me with the graffiti
Watch it, now they'll also put a price tag on me!

A Sand Castle

With child's fingers
let me pick up stones
be perplexed by
black   brown   white   and yellow
Perseus must have passed this way
with Medusa's head
I look at Poseidon's blue canvas
Chrysaor rising
on the plains of my heart
the Tandava of words
Yes, in this inclement Nun
I've been warned of Hathor's horror
Let Ahalya's pining
awaiting a millennium
frozen in Nun
unfold in my palms
Let life have Rama's touch
A skin-to-skin song
The sound, the stone
Let me throw that stone
black, brown
white, yellow
at your glass house
Then, in the primordial chaos
I shall return
to the sanctuary of my sand-castle
to allow
the wind
the sea
the earth
the fire
and the sky
to begin a new song

An Alien

In the country I was born, Alien
In the motherland, Alien
In the land of citizenship, Alien
In the skin, Alien
In the languages, Alien
In the cultures, Alien
In the religion, Alien

Even though
I am a Freeman of the City of London
'They' truly hold the Freedom of Speech

Typical Mr Patel's Typical Promotion

Mr Patel, you're blah blah blah.
BUT.
Can you fill this form for equal opportunity?
It's to allow us to monitor you know what.
Thank you. We'll let you know in due course.
(Never)

Mr Patel,
Sorry,
You were one of the two selected;
BUT.
(Hell, you smell of masala)
Try again next year. (And the year after,
and after, and after.)
Thank you for your interest in our company.

The calf butted the oak:
Mr Patel bought the company
and promoted himself.

A Time Bomb

My skin is not your trophy
It will not hang on your walls
My skin is not a language
It will not dance on your tongue
My skin is not a horse
It will not make a saddle for you
My skin is not the 'me'
It will not be your punch bag
My skin is not a heart
It will not break as you wish

I am thick skinned

My skin is a time bomb

Tick tock, tick tock, tick tock...

A White Paper and a Black Blot

words aren't black ink
a paper can't think

the moon is vulgar
the sun, a pot smoker

It all happens in a day
A ray screws you up
that bloody, bloody ray of hope
the blot now dry, black, and solid

the paper pompously stands up as god
the ink shouts down as 'Sahib'

but the blot knows
God was never a paper, nor an ink

who will tell god
a headline is nothing but His fart?

Home

Only if Abhimanyu knew!
The name of the seventh war zone is
London

And even if there's was a way back to the womb
Krishna
has nothing more to say

Crow

There is a crow on the roof
looking around for flesh
he cares little for mere skin
when you see a man
looking at your skin, not at you
you begin to love the crow

the crow knows
that flesh is better than skin

(From *The Manikin in Exile*)

A Crow without Skin

The bones he had
Brahma forgot the gift of skin
The darkness brushed his face
The Nun filled his skull
The dying Jatayu still struggles for life in his heart
The rotten, diseased flesh was Hades' gift
The smell too
A lift in Amen-Re's boat of "millions of years" was his
hopelessness
Osiris's Judgement too
Still, Brahma's creation without a skin

He lives like a hissing wind
in the gorges of the bones
He looks outside the bone
to find the words
but the words had slipped from Idi Amin's lips

They know he is a crow
He may be born British
But that's why he is all skin
            A coconut – he pretends he hasn't one
Poor fellow, he doesn't know
Enoch Powell will still weave one for him
After all, no skin, no headlines, no Enoch Powells

Brahma also forgot to tell the crow
'Bones and flesh have no meaning
Religion, skin and farting words:
They are real'

A Rescue

I have walked infinite distances
with a burden of the sea
on my back

I dropped it on the sun
and returned home

We both now have a fire put out
sun and me

Please dispatch birds now
to rescue us
to pick us up like straws

from the depth of the seas
I never emptied!

The Sea

The sea undulates as a playful breeze, a slag
amuses itself cuddling the flirting shroud-flag

Putting a head through the wall
stares a mirage-struck stag
Drips from its eyes a sterile language, a shrill
These walls on tenterhooks are a bulwark futile
The mounting sea effuses in
drowning in the engulfing sand
Heaven and earth I move to make the sea understand
Alas, to no end!

At the edge of a village pond
a ripe rose apple is a sea's song
Rushing to the window, I stretch my hand
to find straws only on the wind's strong hand
Holding it, I sink almost conned
The mounting sea effuses in locking me
in its hollow chest
Heaven and earth I move to make the sea understand
Alas, to no end!

Hollow, unrealised, vagabond and sweet: the sea
billows
Like a lover of a one night stand leaving me flat as
skies

Just Try to Touch the Sea

Just try to touch the sea
then only you'll know
how big a sky is
behind your walls!

Then facing the sky
instead of worrying about your being
if you explore the void
like a bird
flying nonchalant
you may find the meaning of the sky
or may give a meaning to the sky!

Even those marooned on the seashore
who have watched the birds
fulfilling their meaning
have never felt
that they are stuck on the seashore

Just try to touch the sea
then only you'll know
how big a sky is
behind your walls!

The Day of the Daffodils

Then they came
as if sperms of the sun had
fallen on the ground one fresh morning

In every wild space
in the open arm fields
in the moaning commons, the lonely greens
the deserted parks and the slumbering gardens
the light itself, the yellow sprang up

Flag bearers of the spring were here
An invasion most welcome was here
Battle lines were drawn
Their fate was already written
On the firing line
they were to fall
as if their job was done
The brief life had an aura
to bridge the rebirth
as if the purpose was served

For only a few days
Yes, yes, they came like every year
religiously
in death to celebrate the awakening
of that tomorrow
the man looking through his glass window
is blind to.

A Can of Coke

A can of Coke
in a reverie
on the seashore...
an attempt to guzzle the sea
a roaring laughter
a kick in the rear from the waves

The sky's bosom
filled with smoke...
a birth, the curse of cultural con
Look, ripping the sky's sari
Duryodhan laughs!
With a blistering arrogance
obliterating the forests
extracting a giant poster
a culture splashes its name across
on the forehead of the city
With the collar on man's neck
this Craven wants to suck the sea
in its gorge
But Poseidon kicks its bottoms
and the arrogance shattered
now licks the sand...

(Winner of the Co-Op Poetry Award on the environment)

Wings

now let me return the wings
my sky is stolen
the bars receive the slap of the flapping wings
I am like a fog; shapeless, nameless
speaking like a gramophone record stuck in a groove

I am a tree with wings
a thing caged
in whiskey of hope

let me return the wings
a tree, a cage, a sky...
Let me throw away the keys

Let me
Let me
Let me

The Sun

Sun, I am returning to you
the asset of these eyes and wings
these promises of a sky
and calls of a horizon
all difficult, strange
Whenever the home seemed near
I had to move
The case of a blade of grass
was the same as mine
They became playthings of the wind

Sun, I am returning to you
a rainbow in the heart of Nun
I am the script of footsteps
I am a fact
erased in ripples

Sun, I am returning to you
the asset of these eyes and wings

(From *The Manikin in Exile*)

The Culture

The sun is a marble
 I'll throw it at you
catch

Like a Speaker's procession
the wind will carry my Mace

The leaves will clap
a hope
Last night's drink glasses
a hope
My game of words
on deaf ears

You may catch the white marble
or walk away from it
or hit it as a Ping-Pong

Just don't give it back to me

Three Droplets

1.

They have all walked
without moving

very few actually have walked with me

2.

It may have been easy
to drink the poison like Shiva
But I am troubled
that to churn the sea
to find Amrit
I still need devils

3

Had no idea when the sea
turned in to a goblet
and I drowned in it...

Words are all Sun now
keep displacing me

I'm needed for my shadow only

All I'm doing is to align myself
so the Sun is pleased

My Reading Glasses

Every morning it's the same old story

I wake up with
a heavy mist of my sleep

from which I see nothing but
a war between a sun and a newspaper

and a cuppa tea
trying to mediate

The news is just in
That they have dragged my body away
to a clock

and my mind
to a morgue

and my heart
to a dead sun

My optimism lies in
not finding my reading glasses
         ever

A Teabag on a Washing Line

Happy as ever I can be
singing
hanging from a washing line
watching
the world undress

listening
a skylark warbling a wild woodnote

What do I care?
Go on let the kettle boil

I have still more life to give

Optimism

I've noticed
in the middle of Kurukshetra
Arjun is scratching his head
God didn't quite explain things
as He did to bin Laden
The reason perhaps
The Bhagavad Gita opens up a maze
all around him

I've noticed
the crow pecks fiercely like a woodpecker
at the Sun every day
A sparrow collects the falling cotton
flutters away to build a nest

The remainder
I've noticed
a lost child collects
to make a pillow

Dozes off
in the middle of a war zone

only to catch a dream

The Outsider

Beyond these walls
these double-glazed windows of words
I stretch my hands
to touch the meadows
shrouded in the chilled silence
of the hate-filled pallid language

The snow is here, this year
early midsummer!
Your gaze

Medusa's eyes
have looked into their hearts
Ahalya pines for the touch of Rama's foot

The albino butterflies
trying to clutch the glass
are the phoney words of promise
trying to touch the warmth

Beyond these walls
these double-glazed windows of words
I stretch my hands
to touch the meadowsweet
to fill the heart with fragrance
shrouded in chilled silence...

Why have they imprisoned me
In this cage?

A bird in me awaits children
to return to Giant's garden
once more
Please do join me then...

An Optimist

Scarab beetle rolls on and on and on
The dung-ball
Ré

All I need is one spark
to light up the dung-ball

Neither Here nor There

The truth has a tail
as ugly as they come

Some like it
Some don't know what to do with it
Others will just stand there in disgust
Some will grab hold of it, swing it
Others will laugh at it, kick it

Oh yes, the truth has a tail all right
pink, slimy, smelly, and sweaty

Some can't see it; bless them
Some will be haunted by it
Some make you see it, even if you can't
Some will just pretend to know it

I wish I was Gandhi
I could own it
Like Congress, sell it
Ask you to buy a stake in it

But I am not black and white
I'm just neither here nor there

Born Again

It was at Heathrow
I was made to realise
I was no longer a human
I was an "alien"
A colour

My blood suddenly was of
future 'Rivers of Blood'
Instantly, I was a bloody number
A threat

The number had no flesh
no face
no values
but it wore a skin
without a human inside
Yes, an alien

I was born in Mombasa once

Heathrow is a second womb
I dropped from

Birth of an alien
in 'Rivers of Blood'

That's why you don't recognise me
Though you were the midwife all along!

You said...

"Bottled Ganges" has an esoteric eastern mystic mystery about it-the poems are redolent with wit and lyric- lines as sinewy as a snake's coils or the widening wanderings of the great river you write of... I know great poetry when I see it!!

Barry Tebb
Editor & Publisher: Sixties Press

'The most striking and remarkable thing about your work is that it is packed with excellent images and enchantment. You have a gift of portraying your feelings through the most original symbols. The balance between the close-ups and long shots is highly commendable... I wish to see you on the top someday......'

Baldev Mirza

You are an exceptional poet. We are proud to have you with us in the pages of The Album of International Poets of Achievement.

Sandra Fowler, Editor: Ocarina, USA

A poem on the sun is a marvellous piece of work.
Isaf Goldman, Editor: Poesie Sonore, Switzerland

His views on poetry, paradoxically, are precise and uncompromising.

Amy Bankier, Wimbledon Guardian

As its name suggests, *Bottled Ganges* offers the reader with a thirst for poetry a refreshing drink that tastes at once familiar and new. Yogesh Patel observes both the mundane and the unexpected, and is fearless in writing what he observes. In his poem, 'Optimism', he writes that 'In the middle of Kurukshetra / Arjun is scratching his head off'! These are poems by an 'outsider' - always a useful perspective in the world of poetry. Patel writes of his alienation 'In the country I was born', in the motherland, and in the land whose citizenship he has embraced, and in so many other contexts. With his typical brand of irony, he ends with the observation that: 'Even though / I am a Freeman of the city of London / "*They*" truly have the Freedom of Speech'. In 'Neither Here Nor There' he comments that truth can be 'As ugly as they come', but no one can shut up this irrepressible poet. His words are important, so let us read, absorb and enjoy.

Dr Debjani Chatterjee, MBE
Writer-in-resident: York St John University

I enjoyed reading your collection of beautiful verses and was moved by the thoughts these conveyed. May I single out, "A Crow Without Skin": The mention of Enoch Powell, the Britishmen and Brahma made my day. Please keep writing. I for one will always enjoy a touch of sarcasm accompanied by reality in many of your poems.

Lord Dholakia of Waltham Brooks OBE DL
Deputy Leader: Liberal Party

I liked The Values, of course, but also God and the Translator and A Dialogue.   I look forward to reading others.

Lord Bhikhu Parekh of Kingston upon Hull
Professor of Political Theory, University of Hull